SO YOU
WANT TO BE
Rich

8 Steps to Personal Success

We are born rich

Published by CreateSpace, a DBA of On-Demand Publishing, LLC.

Printed in the United States of America 2017 - 1st Edition
Cover Design By Stephen Reid, IG: @bleugorilla
Images by www.pexels.com and www.google.com/images
Interior Format and Design by Ana Esther of Es3lla Designs

Library of Congress Cataloging-in-Publications Data
So You Want to be Rich/Stephen Reid

ISBN   978-1-542418-73-7 (pbk.)

1. Reid, Stephen 2. Inspirational 3. Purpose 4. Self-Help
5. Christianity 6. Religious 7. Spirituality 8. Balance

CON**TENTS**

I would like to dedicate my first book to Yazmine, Angel & Jordyn. You can accomplish anything you put your mind to.

FOREWORD

Life takes us in many directions. There are so many facets of both the ordinary and extraordinary. With this in mind, we occasionally connect with those that are a rare find. Those that help us to no longer have a myopic view of life but one that will awaken our senses and catapult us as trailblazers; in our lives, our families, our communities and for generations that will follow.

I can truly say, Stephen is that rare find. I met Stephen several years ago. An indelible impression. A multi-talented individual. At the conclusion of our meeting, I surmised his gifts and talents would surely open doors.

Remarkably, adding to his repertoire of gifts and talents, Stephen succinctly engages the reader--- and without reservation, it is the consummate of all perspectives of this desire 'to be rich.' However, being 'rich' isn't just about financial gains. In this book, Stephen will expand on the negative mindset that can catastrophically halt your progress.

Similarly, do we have the fortitude within to not allow the vicissitudes of life to minimize our goals and realize our dreams? Often times we not only minimize, we eradicate every dream, plan and goal. Echoing in my heart and mind, 'as he thinks in his heart, so is he...' *Proverbs 23:7*.

An excerpt from this profound publication and so eloquently stated, "This book isn't solely about money. It has a lot to do with how you value and believe in yourself, your goals and your talents. If it means something to you, then don't let it go to waste. Don't just spend the cheapest amount of money you can, to improve or maintain it. It has a lot to do with how you value and believe in yourself, your goals and your talents."

And yet another excerpt, "Without hard work, nothing grows but weeds. Therefore once we realize our talents, visions and dreams, we have to work and push ourselves to perfect our craft. To just sit on the things we possess within, is equivalent to hiding a priceless treasure and losing the map. Even we ourselves can't benefit from it."

Without reservation and hesitation, this is a must read. It will engage your thoughts and help you to recognize and realize the many gifts, talents and dreams that have been placed on the inside of each of us before we were born.

As I summarize, rarely do you find someone who is immensely dedicated in exposing us to the reality of true success. Stephen has tapped into the purpose, the plan, the pace that God has for those who desire to follow the necessary steps to be successful in every aspect of life.

Bishop George C. Searight,
Senior Pastor,
Abundant Life Family Worship Church
New Brunswick, NJ.

LET'S CHANGE
YOUR MINDSET
AND GET YOU
OFF OF LIFE'S PATIO

PRE**FACE**

In this technical world where we can find nearly anything on YouTube, I came across a video one day of two men and a dog, entitled *"Dog Won't Walk Through Door Fail."* Envision with me what I saw on this video. There were two men standing on the inside of a patio with french doors. These patio doors had the glass panels removed so that both men were able to walk in and out without opening the doors; Instead they could just step through the open holes where the glass would have been. There was a dog outside that the two men were beckoning to enter the patio. Even though they showed him that there was no glass in the doors, the dog would not enter the patio until the doors were actually opened, as that was the only way he knew to enter the house. To further prove to the dog that it was safe, after letting him in by opening the doors, the men closed the doors and exited the patio by stepping through the space where the glass was removed. Now the dog was confused. He was again locked out (or in) and couldn't exit because of his understanding that no one can physically walk through glass.

Often times, we are left in the same predicament as the dog in this video. You know that there is so much more to accomplish, but past experiences or learned behaviors ultimately block you from reaching your full potential.

You're not smart enough. You're overweight and lazy. You don't have enough money to pay for college or get a business started. These are all barriers we find ourselves facing and just like the dog, you usually don't create your own barriers but if you feed into them they can be the very thing that holds you back and prevent you from walking through open doors.

"For as he thinketh in his heart, so is he…"
Proverbs 23:7a, KJV

You may be familiar with a popular internet image that shows a horse being tied to a chair. This horse just knows that usually he's tied to something heavy or strong enough to keep him from moving. Just like the dog, his mind creates the barrier that tells him that he is not free to move. These barriers are battles in the mind that you can learn to change and overcome. Once you win the battle in your mind you will see just who God has called you to be.

With that in mind, think back to a time or age when the sky was the limit. For a lot of us, that was more or less around twelve to fourteen years old. Some of us wanted to be in the army, some firefighters, some doctors, some in the NFL or NBA, and almost everyone pictured themselves as millionaires living in a fancy house, driving their desired car(s)...but what happened?

Studies show that in 2014, only 4-5% of American households fell into the millionaire category. That's about 1 in every 20 people. At some point, we became that dog in the video and our life experiences became the glass panels. When I say *So You Want To Be Rich,* I'm not just speaking monetarily. Money is not the ultimate goal or measurement, as we should look to obtain *richness* in health, wealth, love, or happiness.

The purpose of this book is not only to remove the glass panels, but to help change your mindset and get you off of life's patio. It's meant to get you to pick back up a pen and write your poetry or music again. Maybe you're a singer and you have settled for just singing at church or in the shower. Perhaps you didn't get drafted out of college, so you've stopped pursuing your dream to become a pro athlete. It could be that you feel like you're too old or out of shape to be that Carnegie Hall dancer, and now is the time to get you on the path to opening your own dance studio. These steps to being *rich* are not the end of the line, but just the mere beginning of the path to being fulfilled and realizing just how rich you truly are.

> *change your mindset and get you off of life's patio.*

INTRO**DUCTION**

When I came up with the title of this book, I imagined many would be drawn to it because of the title alone. Who can blame them? If there were certain steps one can take to become rich, why not know them and apply them, right? Let me first break down what it truly means to be *rich*. Webster's dictionary defines *rich* as:

1. *Possessing great wealth*
2. *Valuable*
3. *Elaborate*
4. *Plentiful and Abundant*

Although these definitions are not tied directly to money, the majority of the world often defines *rich* as financial success and power, political favor, social influence and acceptance, and even military power. There is nothing wrong with these definitions of rich or richness, however the purpose of this book is to bring you to the realization of being truly *rich* through Christ.

"There is one who makes himself rich, yet has nothing; and one who makes himself poor, yet has great riches." Proverbs 13:7 NKJV

Contrary to the more accepted thoughts and definitions on being rich, this book is not all about chasing and obtaining money and objects. Though the principles in this book can and will lead to increases in finances, success, and relationships; chasing and obtaining these things are not the *"rich"* we are shooting for. This book lives on the belief that being truly *rich* is the capability to use the power and things that God has placed inside each of us to become spiritually, mentally, and physically *rich*. These riches are used to bless those around us and ultimately, draw men and women to God's kingdom.

"But seek ye first the kingdom of God, and his righteousness; and all these things shall be added unto you." Matthew 6:33 KJV

God just wants ALL of our attention and He will exceed in providing our wants and needs. He didn't create us to live a mediocre life, but to live life in abundance and victory. The scripture in Matthew referenced above says "and ALL these things shall be added" to us. This is the point where we are truly rich, lacking for nothing. Though some may read this book and think it is easier said than done to begin to think rich, honestly, it really is that simple.

AMERICAN DREAMING

In today's society, we hear names such as Steven Jobs, Oprah Winfrey, Mark Zuckerburg and Bill Gates -- All of whom have made billions of dollars pursuing their dreams and visions. The American Dream is the suggestion that anyone living in the United States has the opportunity to live happy, successful and rich lives through the means of hard work and a quality education. We have the opportunity to pursue our dreams, talents, and careers.   Sometimes as christians, we refer to scriptural clichés such as, "I can do all things", "get your inheritance" and "the wealth of the wicked". Used in the right way they can motivate and encourage us, but they are often overused and become overlooked or just said because they sound good. Contrary to the positive message and words given to us directly from God himself, we often expect and find ourselves living below our potential. We barely tap into our abilities, but rather get frustrated at our regular 9 to 5 job, living paycheck to paycheck, or may be unemployed and hopelessly job searching.

"What lies behind us and what lies before us are tiny matters compared to what lies within us." Ralph Waldo Emerson

At times, we fail to realize that the answers to our prayers for financial help, and more importantly the keys to living rich, have already been placed within us by God. Many of us have talents, visions and dreams that were given to us by God before we were born; Things that have the potential to give us the financial success and satisfaction we want. All too often these things lie dormant or inactive and go with us to our graves.

YOU DON'T HAVE TO TAKE MY WORD FOR IT

Now, just to be clear, in no way am I claiming to know all or have found some great hidden scriptures that give the secrets of living a rich life. But I have allowed several influences including *Super Rich* by Russell Simmons, *Every Day a Friday* by Joel Osteen, *Reposition Yourself* by T.D. Jakes, *the Bible* and words of inspiration from God, to guide my pen on enlightening my fellow Christian brothers and sisters on what it means to be rich. Join me on this path to truly living this way.

> *"It is better to trust in the Lord than to put confidence in man."* Psalms 118:8 NKJV

"It is better to trust in the Lord than to put confidence in man." Psalms 118:8 NKJV

I am a firm believer that you are better off trusting God, than putting confidence in man. So to take away the focus on the "man" writing this book, I constantly offer validation with the truth of scriptures from God's word, *The Holy Bible.* The majority of scriptures come from the book of Proverbs. It was written by King Solomon, one of the richest and wisest men to walk the face of the earth. Who better to learn and take advice from than a man who understood and lived what it means to be truly rich from the inside out? My hope is that you are ready to adjust your thinking and actions as we take this journey towards a rich life. LET'S GO!

STEP**ONE**

ALWAYS GIVE AND YOU WILL ALWAYS HAVE

In order to fully grasp this concept, you must understand that to be rich is not just a financial achievement, but it

> to be rich is not just a financial achievement, but it also means to not lack for anything.

also means to not lack for anything. We rely on many of the luxuries around us on a day-to-day basis. If someone super glued our hands to our cellphones, although anger may be our first reaction, most likely, we would not mind and even be grateful. The cell phone has become such a source of dependency in our world that many people cannot function without it and would even go crazy if not able to find it. Statistics reveal that approximately 9-11% of functional adult Americans still live without a cell phone to this day. Prior to 1973, when the first mobile call was made, there were thousands of years with effective communication. From messengers on horseback, to pigeons, and even smoke signals, a cell phone made things easier and more convenient but was not a necessity. This statement, can also be said for your car, name brand clothes and shoes, computers, tablets, and even most of our food choices. As a child I did not always have the name brand shoes or clothes, because my parents simply could not afford it. However, I cannot say that my parents let me go without being dressed.

One of my favorite commercial photographers shoots everyone from rapper 50 Cent to children in costumes on Halloween. I had the opportunity to watch one of his amazing behind the scene videos. This video documented his travels deep into the rainforest to photograph a secluded village of people for *National Geographics.* The people were detached from what we would call modern civilization. They had very limited use of the things we use almost everyday. One thing in this village that they did have was happiness. The people there had a sense of peace, and an assurance that they were taken care of. With food coming from the river and clothing from the forest, they were in the greatest of spirits. Without money, possessions, and amenities these people were *rich.*

Once you realize God is your source, you will begin to see that your richness does not lie in your bank account but rather, in your heart, mind and spirit. Upon realizing that all of your needs are met, it will be easier for you to integrate the practice of giving. By beginning to give from your heart, (in love, and not expecting a reward or gift in return from man, but putting your trust in God) you will understand that He will see your giving as pure and reward you greatly. As Lavar Burton would say on one of my favorite childhood TV shows, *Reading Rainbow,* "You don't have to take my word for it." The following scriptures show you how a giving spirit and heart is a prerequisite for blessings and prosperity.

GIVE FIRST TO GOD

"Honor the Lord with thy substance, and with the first fruits of all thine increase: So shall thy barns be filled with plenty, and thy presses shall burst out with new wine." Proverbs 3:9 (KJV)

First and foremost, the Bible commands us to give our tithe (10%) to God. The first fruits of all our increase belong to God because without Him our increase would be impossible. It also tells us that in doing so, our barns will be filled with plenty and our vats will overflow.

One way that I like to explain it is if your friend allows you to borrow his or her car. When you are finished using it, you might make sure it is washed, cleaned and the tank is filled with gas. Then you would return the keys. So to relate this to God and tithing, our jobs or increase is His blessing us, "borrowing the car", so we can take care of our needs. Returning those keys are like paying tithes because we are giving God what belongs to Him. The money for gas and washing the car is our offering to show our gratitude. What many of us are guilty of is giving the gas money (our offering) but keeping the keys (our tithe). In order to take the first step in giving, let's honor God by giving him the first fruits of our labor and increase. If you are in a position where you don't have a job, honor God with your time and talents. Some examples of this are volunteering at the local nursing home or homeless shelter or helping clean your church. God will honor our efforts. Remember, true giving comes from the heart.

"Give, and it shall be given unto you; good measure, pressed down, shaken together, and running over, shall men give into your bosom. For with the same measure that ye mete withal it shall be measured to you again."
Luke 6:38 KJV

In having a spirit of giving, we are not only speaking monetarily. It can be giving a helping hand, giving a ride, giving food or even giving free advice. God gives us increase in knowledge, strength, finance or possessions not to hold on to for ourselves, but to share and bless others around us. Theodore Roosevelt once said, "people don't care how much you know until they know how much you care." By having a giving spirit you can show that you care and open the doors to showing what you know and believe about God.

Whenever we give with good measure, we will receive a running over reward in return. As an example of giving with good measure and the right heart, I often look at Genesis 4:3, the infamous story of Cain and Abel. Here you have two brothers, both of whom gave offerings to God. Abel was blessed and God smiled down on his offering. However his older brother, Cain, did not get the same response from God because his offerings were not pure and from the heart. This caused Cain to become jealous of Abel which led him to murder his brother.

What I learned about giving from this story is that if you give with the 'right' heart, you will be blessed in abundance and smiled upon by God allowing us to obtain His favor. Giving with the right heart means giving purely just to give, expecting nothing in return. We should not focus on what we will get in return for that thinking only leads to poverty, curses and even death. We should focus on giving with the right heart so that we can receive all that God has in store for us.

PROJECT GIFT CARDS

"He that hath a bountiful eye shall be blessed; for he giveth of his bread to the poor." Proverbs 22:9 KJV

As I stated, giving is not always about passing out money. I often come across people outside of public places that ask for money to buy food. My habit is to always give if I am capable of doing so, but there are people who disagree and turn the other shoulder when approached by people in need. In many cases they feel that their donation for food will go towards alcohol or drugs which, although unfortunate, is often the case. The way I look at this is, as long as you give and plant the seed with a good heart, it is not up to you to decide where the money goes. Rightfully so, many argue with that train of thought, saying you are just supporting bad habits. So in using discernment and Godly wisdom, I came up with the solution of using gift cards. For this purpose, I keep a number of gift cards with money on them. Now at any given time I can bless someone without having to worry where the money went. This also works well because, like many people, I seldom carry cash on me. I found this to be a perfect solution. Now when approached and I bless them with a gift card they are grateful because we both know the next couple of meals are taken care of for that person.

"Be not forgetful to entertain strangers, for thereby, some have entertained angels unawares." Hebrews 13:2 (KJV)

One late night, which actually was about 3 o'clock in the morning, I was making a late night run to the 24-hour Walmart. I was on my way back and thinking about nothing more than getting home and in the bed. I was almost home when I passed a young guy who was in the middle of the road. I watched as other drivers swerved to get around him. His car apparently stalled and he was struggling to push the car off the road by himself. I couldn't ignore the voice of God that said to "stop and help this young man". After helping him to the nearest parking lot, the guy explained he ran out of gas. I gave him a little cash to get a gas can and gas from the nearest gas station. He asked for my name. Once I told him, he said, "Thanks, my name is Angel." It was at that moment I knew God was just telling me to continue helping and giving to others because His 'angels'

> *It was at that moment I knew God was just telling me to continue helping and giving to others because His 'angels' are certainly in place. You never know if the person you are entertaining was put in place by God to test you and your purity of your giving.*

are certainly in place. You never know if the person you are entertaining was put in place by God to test you and your purity of your giving.

When we go to our jobs, we expect to get paid. As believers, we have to give with the same expectation that God will repay and help us to continue to be a blessing to others. He will even send help in our time of need. So work the faith it takes to give to someone knowing he/she cannot repay you, and you can expect a reward from God.

EVEN MY ENEMIES?

"If thine enemy be hungry, give him bread to eat; and if he be thirsty, give him water to drink: For thou shalt heap coals of fire upon his head, and the Lord shall reward thee." ~ Proverbs 25:21-22 KJV

Giving doesn't just mean to the poor or needy; one can be a blessing to your pastor, friends and family, strangers and yes, even our enemies! I like to look at the following passage that Jesus spoke in Luke 6:27-36(KJV):

"But I say unto you which hear, Love your enemies, do good to them which hate you, bless them that curse you, and pray for them which despitefully use you. And

unto him that smiteth thee on the one cheek offer also the other; and him that taketh away thy cloke forbid not to take thy coat also. Give to every man that asketh of thee; and of him that taketh away thy goods ask them not again. And as ye would that men should do to you, do ye also to them likewise. For if ye love them which love you, what thank have ye? for sinners also love those that love them. And if ye do good to them which do good to you, what thank have ye? for sinners also do even the same. And if ye lend to them of whom ye hope to receive, what thank have ye? for sinners also lend to sinners, to receive as much again. But love ye your enemies, and do good, and lend, hoping for nothing again; and your reward shall be great, and ye shall be the children of the Highest: for he is kind unto the unthankful and to the evil. Be ye therefore merciful, as your Father also is merciful."

Jesus tells us, as believers we will encounter those who will hate, curse, use, and steal from us. Naturally, knowing the thoughts and intentions of some people, we could be tempted to not give to them. Instead, God commands us to do good, bless, pray for, and continually give to everyone. And to do so in love. Anyone can bless someone who loves them and lend to those who will repay us. The challenge is, we must keep a mindset that as long as we give from our hearts our reward is not returned to us from man, but from God who will provide for us as his children.

LOVE THEM, ANYWAY

People are often unreasonable, illogical, and self-centered.
Forgive them anyway.
If you are kind,
people may accuse you of selfish ulterior motives.
Be kind anyway.
If you are successful,
you will win some false friends and some true enemies.
Succeed anyway.
If you are honest and frank,
people may cheat you.
Be honest and frank anyway.
What you spend years building,
someone could destroy overnight.
Build anyway.
If you find serenity and happiness,
they may be jealous.
Be happy anyway.
The good you do today,
people will often forget tomorrow.
Do good anyway.
Give the world the best you have,
and it may never be enough.
Give the best you've got anyway.
You see,
**in the final analysis it is between you and God;
it was never between you and them anyway.**
Mother Teresa

Mother Teresa was another great follower of Christ who believed and shared this same belief concerning giving. She realized that the final judgment ultimately comes from God. No matter what man does to us, it can't grant nor deny us access into heaven. God judges us and He knows our hearts, therefore He looks at how we treat others from our hearts with unconditional love. As you are reading this, I challenge you to find an opportunity to just simply give. Do you know what it feels like to just GIVE a $100, $500, or even $1,000 not expecting it back in return? Bless a church. Bless a stranger. You will not regret it because God will bless you.

STEP**TWO**

BELIEVE IN YOURSELF THROUGH CHRIST

FAITHFUL TO BELIEVE

One of the dictionary's definitions of faith is "complete confidence in a person or plan." Faith is one of the most powerful weapons we have. In order to begin to live *rich*, we must have faith or confidence in ourselves or the abilities within. Arnold Schwarzenegger said that when he was a kid, they had little money, clothes, food and no television, but he was still rich because he had a dream.

Where would we be if Lydia Newman had not invented the hairbrush as we know it? Where would we be if the Wright Brothers had not taken the first flight in 1903? What about one of my personal favorite developments, peanut butter? How would I have survived this long in life had George Washington Carver Jr. not creatively made use of peanuts? Would we still be in the dark if Thomas Edison had given up on developing the light bulb? What if these men and women listened to people who said they were crazy? What if they could not see past the norm of what already existed? Before anyone could believe or come to know these great achievers as inventors or people in history books, first, they had to have faith and confidence in their knowledge and ability to succeed.

"The man who thinks he can and the man who thinks he cannot are both right." ~Henry Ford

The most common difference between achieved and unachieved goals, is the lack of belief or faith in oneself. Believing in yourself gives you the power to work through failure and rejections, while giving you the ability to dig deep within yourself and pull out greatness. For example, when we look at sports, the underdog finds a way to win for no reason other than they believe they can, and refuses to accept failure. In the movie, *Rudy,* the main character knew he could play football one day for Notre Dame, despite his size, speed, and level of talent. He tried to enroll into Notre Dame for years but he didn't have the grades to get accepted into the school. Not only did his family doubt him but his fellow teammates and coaches did not believe that he had "what it took" to be in uniform and on the field during a game. His undeniable faith in himself ultimately made others believe and envision what he could do to the point where starting players were willing to give up their uniforms just to see Rudy on the field. When he finally got a chance to play, he made an awesome defensive play at the end of a big game and his family, teammates, and everyone in the stadium chanted his name. Everyone believed in him. This universal undeniable belief would not have been possible if he didn't first believe in himself. There are hundreds of thousands of books, movies, and real life stories that reaffirm this point. There is not one champion who just wakes up on the winner's podium. Being empowered by God and believing in themselves, they allow for hard work, determination, failures, and sometimes countless sleepless nights to push them to their maximum potential.

"I can do all things through Christ which strengthens me." Philippians 4:13

Now to take belief in self a little further, Christ Himself came to this earth and conquered ALL things, even death. If you truly take on the attributes of Christ, through Him there is nothing you can not accomplish. It is your responsibility to give it to Him in prayer and do your part, for faith without works is indeed dead. (James 2:20)

"And Jesus answering saith unto them, Have faith in God. For verily I say unto you, That whosoever shall say unto this mountain, Be thou removed, and be thou cast into the sea; and shall not doubt in his heart, but shall not doubt in his heart, but shall believe that those things which he saith shall come to pass; he shall have whatsoever he saith. Therefore I say unto you, What things soever ye desire, when ye pray, believe that ye receive them, and ye shall have them." ~ Mark 11:22-24

It definitely takes a certain level of faith to be able to move mountains. What Jesus wants us to see is that through Him, all things are obtainable, no matter what odds (mountains) are against us.

Imagine you were just a child making your way into the Oval Office to tell the President that you can single handedly defeat a country's army that has been destroying and scaring our military. This is exactly what happened in one of my favorite passages in the Bible. David was a young boy when he came to the battle grounds to bring his older brothers food. He heard and answered the challenge of the Philistines' greatest and also biggest champion, Goliath. David approaches King Saul as being the right man for the job and the King is unsuccessful at persuading David otherwise. Although he's young, David has faith in God and himself. He tells King Saul how he has killed lions and bears and that all he needs is his sling and 5 stones. Confident in his abilities, he took Goliath down and literally took the head of this eight to ten foot tall giant.

There are many wonderful things I admire and take from young David. The first being, believe in yourself through Christ. His confidence was so strong that it overpowered any doubts or fears, even when the King said it could not be done. This reminds me of the scene in the movie, *The Pursuit of Happyness,* where Chris Gardner played by Will Smith told his son, "Don't let anyone ever tell you that you can not do something, including me." So like Rudy and young David, you have to know beyond any doubt that no matter the circumstance, you are the "one" for the job.

Another point to address is that once young David convinced the King he was the man for the job, King Saul offered him a soldier's armor and weapons. David knew he was not trained in this equipment and it was too heavy for him. From this I glean this revelation:, know your lane, and have confidence in your tools and/or abilities. Do not try to imitate the talents and abilities of others because it can simply be too heavy of a weight to bare and will cost you to ultimately stumble.

> *Do not try to imitate the talents and abilities of others because it can simply be too heavy of a weight to bare and will cost you to ultimately stumble.*

If you know that you have played quarterback all your life and your body is built for the position, then do not try to get to the NFL playing the position of a linebacker. If you have been writing poetry and music all your life then why break into the industry as a DJ, only because the DJ at the local club has fun doing it and you may know how to manage your iTunes playlist. If you have understood and been interested in politics all your life and you want to run for President, then don't aim to be in the NBA. Although, President Barack Obama has a nice jump shot, he chose to focus himself in an area of greater passion. Pay attention to what God has placed in your heart, believe in yourself and follow through. Avoid trying something because King Saul is telling you that, "Everyone is wearing this new soldier equipment and it looks good on you." You must believe in and know yourself.

In convincing King Saul that he could indeed do the job, he confidently shared his skills that he had developed as a shepherd. He had faced bears and lions while protecting his father's sheep. So what I am telling you is, use everything to your advantage as you move through life. Being on a team with a no nonsense leader might have prepared you for a summer internship with a difficult boss and/or co-workers. That summer internship will prepare you to be the boss or CEO of your own corporation, just as David eventually took Saul's position.

Lastly, remember David was not initially going to fight when he recognized there was an opportunity to use his skillset. He believed in himself enough to answer a call even though no one took him into consideration. In God's bigger picture, it was his call to answer and he was positioned to be right where he needed to be. Sometimes we need to be prepared to respond to unexpected opportunities.

For instance, you may be out getting lunch for the office and someone presents an opportunity that you have been waiting for. You never created business cards because you didn't think you were ready, or you did not record and put yourself on YouTube because you could not decide what to sing. God is intentional in moving things around and aligning the right people in our path. "Faith without works is dead." You may find through small talk you are sitting next to a writer or publisher on the train, yet you never began writing the book God placed on your heart. If you would only believe in yourself through Christ and always be prepared and ready for opportunities, you will be amazed at how God moves.

THE OTHER SIDE OF FEAR

Believing in yourself through Christ also requires a level of commitment towards conquering your fears. A lot of times we are held back from our visions and dreams simply because we are scared and afraid of the unknown or even scared of what the results may be.

TWO DOTS

There is an addictive puzzle game that I downloaded on my phone entitled "Two Dots." It's a fairly simple puzzle game, where you connect two or more dots of the same color to clear each level. The game would be boring if each level didn't present some sort of challenge. I have had so much fun playing the game that I asked several friends to download the game and see how many levels they could beat. Over a small period of time, I was well past level 100. Likewise, almost everyone else that played was progressing at pretty much the same rate. I had one friend in particular who was stuck somewhere between levels 25 and 30. She actually got to a point where she couldn't play anymore. When I asked why, she told me that the fire levels gave her too much anxiety. As I mentioned before, each level has its challenges and this fire that was giving her a panic was indeed one of those challenges. As the player tries to reach the color goals for the level, some of the dots ignite into flames. When I first played, it seemed as if the fire was random and based on speed so I rushed to complete the goals, which forced me to think and strategize quickly. This was not an impossible feat but with that train of thought I could see where the anxiety came from. As I stuck with it, I began to realize, *I can control the fire.* The fire only spreads when I made a move, so instead of feeling rushed, I strategically moved around the board to put the fire out. After realizing this, I was no longer held up by the obstacle. As for my friend, it took a couple of days of convincing her to get over her fear and conquer the fire before she eventually realized that she controls the fire that was controlling her fear. The next time we discussed her progress in the game she was close to passing my level. She literally, was taken to another level on the other side of her fear. So can you!

DARKNESS TO LIGHT

"For God hath not given us the spirit of fear…" 2 Timothy 1:7

One of the most innovative and inventive minds we have had on this earth was Thomas Edison. Not a day goes by that we don't use or are around something that this great mind has a patent on. Even though he accomplished more than the average person, he was still human. With that being said, Thomas Edison was actually afraid of the dark. I have read that Mr. Edison would fall asleep with all the lights on. Even when he died, all the lights were on in the house. Now, many people know or associate Edison with the light bulb and though he didn't invent it himself, he invented a way that it could become a household item and stay lit for longer periods of time. What a lot of people also don't know is Edison also invented the phonograph and recorded and played back some of the first sounds of human voices. To me, this invention was just as conquering and victorious as the first mentioned invention of the incandescent light bulb because Edison was deaf or going deaf as well.

So many times we are at the brink of an opportunity, on the verge of success, or some of us have even received words from God, but we allow our fears and handicaps to create doubt that prevents us from reaching our goals and dreams. Looking back at my friend, the cell phone game was controlling her fear, and once she realized that she could control the fire, she was able to overcome her anxiety and continue playing the game. Once you face and conquer your fears you will literally grow and be taken to new levels. As for Mr. Edison, his determination pushed him past his fears, weaknesses and handicaps, and landed him a prime spot in our history books. He literally used power and a sound mind to conquer fear.

LIMITED

VS

STANDARD

LIMITED VS. STANDARD

Another example is Michael Jordan. Despite current efforts by Lebron James and Steph Curry, in my eyes, he is still one of the greatest players in the history of the National Basketball Association (NBA). Not only because he has physically achieved things no other player in his field has, but his statistics, records and championship wins still reign amongst the long list of those trying to have a career close to his. I mean, the guy led his Chicago Bulls to a three-peat (winning three championships back to back) after coming out of a brief retirement where he went and played baseball. Before this becomes a Jordan biography chapter, let me get to the point.

In Jordan's 15-year NBA career, he made anywhere from ninety-one to ninety-four million dollars. However, with his Jordan shoes and brand under Nike, Mike currently makes approximately one-hundred million dollars a year. Not so bad for the retired ball player huh? Unfortunately, I do think that is a little bad for everyone else. As a whole, Americans tend to spend money on things that don't give us much in return.

Let me explain it this way. In the movie *Baby Boy*, Ving Rhames said it best, in one of my personal favorite scenes. He basically said our problem is that we just don't get it. We make money and know how to be entrepreneurs but still fail to understand Rhames' version of "Guns and Butter." Guns are the things such as real estate, stocks and bonds, things that appreciate with value. Butter are the things like Jordans sneakers that have a value that melts away once you buy it. Now I'm not saying go out and spend all your money in stocks and art or whatever will gain monetary value, but I am saying consider investing in yourself. The monetary value of a book would definitely be in the butter category but when compared to the value of knowledge and insight, it easily can fall under the guns category.

In 2015, Americans spent over $70.15 *billion* on lottery tickets, that same year we only spent $32.18 *million* on printed and digital books. To put that in perspective, books on average can cost anywhere from $3.99 to $25 or sometimes more. While lottery tickets are only a dollar or two. Nothing against the lottery at all, heck we all could use an extra couple million in the bank. However, the question remains, how much are you investing in yourself? If your goal is to have good health and a nice body, why not calculate how much you spend on eating out and on junk foods and use that money to pay someone to prepare your healthy meals on a weekly basis? Or perhaps instead of the ten to twenty dollars a month you spend on snacks, use it to join the local gym or fitness club. If you're an aspiring photographer, real estate agent or hairstylist, why not spend a little money on a couple of good books, webinars or conferences to help you perfect your craft to expand and reach your goals?

Tai Lopez put it this way, "whatever you have is what you deserve." Meaning, you may hate the way you look in the mirror, but it is the body that you deserve. You know how much you workout and what you eat. You may hate your job or position, but are you putting in the extra hours to get a promotion or are you doing just enough every day for the end of the day to come? It has a lot to do with how you value and believe in yourself, your goals and your talents. If it means something to you, then don't let it go to waste. Don't just spend the cheapest amount of money you can, to improve or maintain it.

"Give not that which is holy unto the dogs, neither cast ye your pearls before the swine…" Matthew 7:6 KJV

What would you do if you found out today that next week Oprah Winfrey, Bill Gates, or President Obama was coming over for dinner? If your mom were anything like mine, you'd be breaking out the best plates and cleaning the house from ceiling to floors. You know that someone of value is on his or her way, so you'd roll out the red carpet treatment. What if you valued yourself with those same standards and invested in yourself with that same kind of effort or mindset? Where would you be able to go and what could you achieve?

I purchased a 2013 Hyundai Sonata Limited Edition with a 2.0 engine. I am no car fanatic so I am not 100% sure what the 2.0 engine meant but I did know that limited was not standard. So every oil change or gas fill up, I invest in the best grades of oil and gas. I want my Hyundai Limited Edition to perform at top performance level. Sure the oil and gas price almost doubles with the amount of gallons it takes to fill up the tank, but they gave me a Limited Edition. Are you standard or limited? Were you destined for greatness or mediocrity? Don't be afraid to simply believe and invest what in you are worth.

STEP**THREE**

NEVER BE LAZY

One late night, while watching The Word Network, I saw a woman give a testimony. She said that God gave her an idea for an invention. The invention was simple enough for her to carry it through without needing loads of startup money. She just simply needed to do it! Instead, she sat on it for days. Quickly those days turned to weeks, the weeks into months and before she knew it, years had gone by. She just so happened to be up late, as I was, watching infomercials. Lo and behold, the exact invention she sat on, was on the television done exactly how she had envisioned. Instead of it being her on the infomercial, it was invented by someone else on the other side of the world. At that moment she could do nothing but cry. She knew she missed out. This story taught me two things, and no, it was not that watching late night television is educational. It taught me the significance of not being lazy, especially when it is something we feel

God is urging in us to do. God's plans and ideas will get done even if you choose not move on them when He tells you to move.

"The soul of the sluggard desireth, and hath nothing: but the soul of the diligent shall be made fat." Proverbs 13:4 KJV

How many people have you entertained that have great ideas? You may even see qualities and potential in them that if exercised, could cause them to live differently. Instead, they sit home 'beating the system' and collecting welfare, unemployment and food stamps. My intent isn't to send out the wrong message. I am not saying there is anything wrong with using these services provided by the government for what it is intended to do; assist in a difficult transition. Everyone has a point and time in life where help is needed in some shape or form. The problem lies with those who use them as a crutch and an excuse to do nothing.

I even think back to the life of young Forrest Gump, his legs were not strong enough to walk properly and he was given braces to help him gain strength. As he grew older, he was ridiculed and had a tough time walking. But God had a different plan, he placed inside Forest the talent of running. One day when being chased and made fun of he was forced to run, and run he did. He ran right out of his braces and into the beginning of his destiny. He not only received a scholarship to college but he became known as a runner.

Despite the outside awkward appearance of the braces that he once needed, on the inside he was built to do great things with his legs.

God often places so much inside of us, answering our prayers of financial increase but we sometimes are too comfortable to get up and be diligent. So in turn, we truly find ourselves with nothing. A little hard work goes a long way. Don't rely on the help you once needed to sustain you into your life's destiny. Dig deep and find the thing that God placed inside of you to run you into your future. With hard work and by eliminating excuses we could easily find ourselves rich; wanting and lacking for nothing.

"The hand of the diligent shall bear rule; but the slothful shall be put to forced labor." Proverbs 12:24 KJV

I know many people who simply do not know how to make it to work, engagements, meetings, rehearsals, and even parties *on time.* I can truly understand that sometimes circumstances such as traffic and weather can delay us, but to be late just because we always have to take that extra five to ten minutes in the bed or shower is not a good habit to have. A lot of times, the ones who are never on time always complain or say they can do their boss' job better if given the chance. They do not realize just how diligent that boss (ruler) is. That he or she is there before the office opens up and also spends countless nights working late after the office has closed. Not to mention the days when they might not show up, they are not on some luxury vacation, but at meetings to keep the company running and ensuring you still have a job to go to. Simply put, if we can begin to show more diligence we just might find ourselves with more ruling positions.

"Go to the ant, you sluggard! Consider her ways and be wise, Which, having no captain, overseer or ruler, provides her supplies in the summer, and gathers her food in the harvest. How long will YOU slumber, O sluggard? When will you rise from your sleep? A little sleep, a little slumber, a little folding of the hands to

sleep- So shall your poverty come on you like a prowler, and your need like an armed man." ~ Proverbs 6:6 KJV

I was once in a position where I could actually sit quietly and watch a few ants. As boring as it may sound or seem, it proved to be very educational. As I was watching the ants, I happened to be eating a turkey sandwich. I decided to shake a few of my crumbs close to them just to observe how they handled it.

In a matter of minutes, the one ant found the scattered crumbs. One by one he picked them up and for a short time disappeared with them. The final piece he couldn't move because it was just too big for him to travel any distance with. I continued watching the ant as he disappeared shortly and returned with two more ants. Together, they picked up the piece and took it away. I was so impressed with their deligence that I gave them a few more crumbs. The scripture (Proverbs 6:6) reminded me so much of this day I watched these ants. A lot of times God can use simple things of nature such as Balaam's ass, to show and teach us a lesson. The ants were in search of food and even they didn't let the size of the job stop them. I was impressed and pleased with their diligence that I blessed their efforts with more. In this situation, God was showing me what it means to be faithful over the few things, so that He will make me ruler over the many.

"What doth it profit, my brethren, though a man say he hath faith, and have not works? Can faith save him? If a brother or sister be naked, and destitute of daily food. And one of you say unto them, Depart in peace, be ye warmed and filled; notwithstanding. Ye give them not those things which are needful to the body; what doth it profit? Even so faith, if it hath not works, is dead, being alone. Yea, a man may say. Thou hast faith, and I have works: shew me thy faith without works, and I will shew thee my faith by my works. Thou believest that there is one God; thou doest well: the devils also believe and tremble. But wilt thou know, O vain man, that faith without works is dead? Was not Abraham our father justified by his works, when he had offered Isaac his son upon the alter? Seest thou how faith wrought with his works, and by works was faith made perfect? And the scripture was fulfilled which saith, Abraham believed God, and it was imputed unto him for righteousness: and he was called the Friend of God. Ye see then how that by works a man is justified, and not by faith only." ~ James 2:14-26 KJV

This passage reminds me of a friend, a fellow brother and believer in Christ, with whom I often played basketball. He always spoke on how much faith he had. He even believed one day God would bring him to the point where he could dunk the ball. I never doubted God could do it. In all the times we played, he could never dunk or even come close to dunking. Then I realized I never seen him even working towards it. I asked him what was he doing to get himself to the point where he can be able to dunk. He answered me saying "just simply believe in God!" Though he was very confident, I'm pretty sure to this day, even if you are picking up this book ten years after I have written and published it, my good brother still has not dunked a basketball on a regulation-sized goal.

We can believe for many things, but without work or effort, all that faith is as good as dead. Even when it comes to making it to heaven and gaining our eternal riches. If we continue to sit in our rooms believing and sleeping, by what works would we have signed our name to that great book on judgment day?

WORK OR WEEDS

Without hard work, nothing grows but weeds. Therefore once we realize our talent, visions and dreams, we have to work and push ourselves to perfect our craft. To just sit on the things we possess within, is equivalent to hiding a priceless treasure and losing the map. Even we ourselves can't benefit from it.

So if you have that screenplay for an award winning movie, your life story in a book, that multi-million dollar invention that will put you in the history books or even a song that God keeps playing in your head to write, just simply do the work. No matter how big the task, God will be pleased and send you help to complete the work He started in you.

"Some people don't try to get better until they are sick."
~Pastor Tracy Davis

Your level of success depends on how proactive you are or aren't. Being a go-getter can make the difference when everyone is just as talented or better. Will Smith said, "you may have more talent than me, you might know more people but you will not out run me on the treadmill." When it comes to reaching our dreams, we are in a very competitive world full of unseen talent. You cannot be lazy and wait for every opportunity to come your way; you have to sometimes make your own opportunities. After all the practice and all the experience, you still have to put yourself in position to reach your goals and dreams. It may just mean moving to Los Angeles because it is

You cannot be lazy and wait for every opportunity to come your way; you have to sometimes make your own opportunities.

better suited to help reach your goal of being an actor, than the small town that you might live in. Your small town surroundings may have served its purpose, but now its time is up. Save up and get your ticket. Steve Harvey said it best, "sometimes you just have to jump and let God catch you, because He will."

STEP**FOUR**

GIVE ALL YOUR TRUST TO GOD

"Every evening I turn my worries over to God. He is going to be up all night anyway." Mary C. Crowley

Putting all your trust in God truly requires handing your total life over to Him. Many of us find ourselves enjoying church and having a love for God, but we never fully give ourselves to Him, or allow ourselves to be IN LOVE with God. For some, the problem lies with being IN LOVE with someone we've never seen.

As women and men, we have been hurt before. We have been damaged by the love we've searched for in relationships. Being in relationships with people we can touch and feel, whether it is familial, romantic or platonic, has all too often let us down. If we are honest, we have been guilty of letting down others at times as well. If we looked at the Bible, this would come as no surprise. Psalms 118:8 teaches us that it is better to put trust in God, than to have confidence in man. So right there in one quick and simple scripture God gave us a solution to avoid being let down. TRUST IN HIM!!! Now you may ask several things. Like how would trusting in God help us not feel the pain of being let down by others.? How will that make me RICH!? As my pastor would often say, "Well, I'm glad you asked."

For those relationships where we have been let down or we have messed up on our own, if we bring our concerns before God daily in prayer, through faith, we avoid being disappointed or making foolish choices. Trusting God in relationships doesn't mean you'll never be let down, but this is not a relationship book, it's about how to be *rich* in its true essence. In taking on the mindset of being *rich*, you will begin to see that it goes hand in hand with improving relationships in your life. I asked you to expand your thinking on these first three concepts and practice them in all aspects of your life. As I write this book, I am constantly reminded of the man who practiced these concepts best, Jesus. The Son of God Himself gave us this same message in a parable.

"Therefore I say unto you, Take no thought for your life, what ye shall eat, or what ye shall drink; nor yet for your body, what ye shall put on. Is not the life more than meat, and the body than raiment? Behold the fowls of the air: for they sow not, neither do they reap, nor gather into barns; yet your heavenly Father feedeth them. Are ye not much better than they? Which of you by taking thought can add one cubit unto his stature? And why take ye thought for raiment? Consider the lilies of the field, how they grow; they toil not, neither do they spin: And yet I say unto you, That even Solomon in all his glory was not arrayed like one of these. Wherefore, if God so clothe the grass of the field, which to day is, and tomorrow is cast into the oven, shall he not much more clothe you, O ye of little faith? Therefore take no thought, saying, What shall we eat? or, What shall we drink? or, Wherewithal shall we be clothed? (For after all these things do the Gentiles seek:) for your heavenly Father knoweth that ye have need of all these things. But seek ye first the kingdom of God, and his righteousness; and all these things shall be added unto you. Take therefore no thought for the morrow: for the morrow shall take thought for the things of itself. Sufficient unto the day is the evil thereof." ~ Matthew 6:25-34 KJV

Jesus was teaching us how to live a *rich* life in these verses. When you can truly realize that you don't have to worry about anything, you learn to trust Him. Through total faith and trust in God, all things are taken care of. You will begin to see that at any given moment, you don't really need anything. A perfect example is that as I write this portion, I am currently in a county jail in New Jersey. I would love to be able to text my friends and family or just get a simple meal to my liking (Applebee's boneless wings). However, they are just flat out considered wants and not needs. Even down to more simple things; I can't wear my choice of clothing but yet I am clothed. Though my surroundings aren't my preference, I have clean air to breath, water to drink, I am of good health and mental awareness. I am in a situation where luxuries have been stripped away from me but I can still retain my joy and be rich because I truly have no worries or wants to be fulfilled. I know God can and will deliver me from my troubles and in the meantime, He will take care of me. Naturally you may question as you're reading this, how can a man in jail feel rich? The following scriptures can confirm that mentality.

"My brethren, count it all joy when ye fall into divers temptations; Knowing this, that the trying of your faith worketh patience. But let patience have her perfect work, that ye may be perfect and entire, wanting nothing." ~ *James 1:2-4 KJV*

"Hearken, my beloved brethren, Hath not God chosen the poor of this world rich in faith, and heirs of the kingdom which he hath promised to them that love him?" ~ *James 2:5 KJV*

To be truly rich is to lack for nothing and putting all trust in God. When that is achieved, the financial blessing will begin to manifest in your life. I once heard a rich man say, "The more money I have, the more free stuff I'm given, so I continue to give as I receive." When you realize that you have everything you need and through Christ you are already rich, it will make it easy for you to not get caught up in material things that you cannot take with you from this world.

"Who is the image of the invisible God, the firstborn of every creature: For by him were all things created, that are in heaven, and that are in earth, visible and invisible, whether they be thrones, or dominions, or principalities, or powers: all things were created by him, and for him: And he is before all things, and by him all things consist."
~ Colossians 1:15-17 KJV

We may trust in an airplane pilot who flies us across the world, a mechanic working on our cars, a doctor to cure us, or trust a lawyer or judge to give us justice. However, I would like for you to think back to the *Matrix Trilogy* movie for a moment. The main character Neo, weather or not he was chosen, he was a regular man that ultimately couldn't do anything until he found the Architect, the man who built it all. Many people are able to find trust on a daily basis due to their professionalism or expertise in something, still it can't compare to the results of the Architect of the world we live in, GOD. All God requires of us is to earnestly seek and trust Him. Just think, it's just that easy without having to swallow a red or blue pill.

"Keep me as the apple of the eye, hide me under the shadow of thy wings, From the wicked that oppresses me, from my deadly enemies, who compass me...Like as a lion that is greedy of his prey, and as it were a young lion lurking in secret places. Arise, O Lord, disappoint him, cast him down: deliver my soul from the wicked, which is thy sword." ~ Psalms 17:8-9, 12-13 KJV

David is showing us that we may have enemies and things that are overcoming or killing us. When we trust God with it, He will arise and smite our enemies with His mighty sword. Often, we try to deal with so much on our own, and inadvertently allow ourselves to be defeated. It's important to realize that our enemy is not always a person, but an opposing force.

Your list of enemies can vary from your bills, job circumstances, relationships, illnesses, social media; anything that challenges where you are trying to go. As you come up against different events on a daily basis, instead of trying to take your problems, stresses, and situations head on or instead of arguing with that co-worker, just keep your focus on God and know that He will rightfully handle your every situation. Just like David realized, God won't step in and force Himself in your business, instead you have to hand it over to Him.

For those who need to see something more practical like sports, let's talk about football. In the 2015 Super Bowl, the Seattle Seahawks got the ball all the way down to the one-yard line and had the game pretty much won. They had one of the strongest and hardest to tackle running backs in the league. Everyone knew that once they got the ball so close to the end zone, it would be an automatic score. However, the coach decided to let the quarterback throw the ball and it was intercepted. They literally threw the game away and lost the Super Bowl. Unlike the game of football where nothing is a sure thing, we have a God that we can hand the ball off to and He will never fail us. We need to be just like David as he knew he could only defeat so many enemies by himself. The Seahawks can only run the ball so far, we can only argue with that nagging coworker or get that car fixed but so many times, before we call on HIM.

STEP**FIVE**

CHOOSE YOUR FRIENDS WISELY

Someone once told me "a negative will always drain a positive." It's just a concept in the universe that almost always proves true. In this chapter we are talking about your circle of friends. Yes, it's good to choose your friends wisely. Here's something to consider. When I was in college, I was a member of the track team. From high school to college, workouts was a tough adjustment. My freshman year I had a good friend named Joe who was my training partner. Every day at 3:00 pm we would curse and complain about going to practice. He would always say to me, "Man, I don't know how we are going to make it through this workout today" or "How do you think coach will kill us today?" And without fail no matter how hard or easy the workouts were, we never would find ourselves able to finish. Until one day Joe didn't come; so I made my way to coaches' office before practice and I asked him, "Coach, what are we doing today?" Though I thought it was a seemingly simple question, his answer was not only positive but pretty much changed the rest of any practices I had in college. He simply told me, "Whatever it is, just know it will make you better!" I thought about it and instead of seeing practice as killing me, I changed my mindset and thought about it as building of my muscles and body, making me faster, stronger, and better. That day I finished practice and ran all the target times or faster. After that day, I began to avoid Joe and his negative words before practices. I began to complete my goals while he would lay out with the "dead" mentality. I felt better than ever. This was an example on how a negative drained the positive and why it is good to choose your friends wisely.

"Do not be deceived: Evil company corrupts good habits." ~1 Corinthians 15:33 KJV

We are witnesses to this scripture so often it's sickening. We constantly hear and see in the media of famous athletes and entertainers who find themselves in serious trouble. The majority of the time, it's not because they are bad people or even because they don't care, but simply because of the company they keep. A lot of times their bank accounts rise but their choice of friends stays the same and/or declines. And the truth of this simple scripture and concept brings to a halt a lot of the successful careers and reputations of these superstars.

"A man who has friends must himself be friendly…" ~ Proverbs 18:24a KJV

A vital part of choosing friends wisely is being able to have friends. And to be successful in life, it is very important to network and build business relationships, as well as friendships. In a competitive world, being friendly may be what separates you from everyone else in your line of business or simply the deciding factor as to why someone chooses to work with you or includes you in business deals. As you go through the day, practice a simple exercise that will almost for sure change your perspective on any situation. *The smile.* Even if at first it is forced, it is almost impossible to stay upset, sad, or in a negative mood if you just bring a smile to the equation. You never know who is watching or who it will attract. Could it be the next big client or million dollar check? Or even better, it may just cause someone else to go from having a bad day to a good one. So remember, no matter what you face or go through, your smile may make the difference.

RICH FRIENDS VS. POOR FRIENDS

As we start to pay attention to who we surround ourselves with or even who you communicate with on a daily basis, another thing you may start to realize is that you have rich friends and poor friends. You have victors and complainers. As you begin to analyze your friends, keep an open mind to who is rich and who is poor. One friend never has money when it's time to hangout, but that same friend may be rich in maintaining a healthy lifestyle; therefore, making them the best motivation and gym buddy. You may have a friend who is awesome with money management and savings, or a friend that keeps romantic and platonic relationships for long periods of time. Pay attention to these details and start to adopt them into your life.

My dad once told me, if you take the positive things from the people you know and apply them to yourself you will be a successful and well-rounded individual. It's because of my dad's consistent and determined early morning prayer life, when I was growing up, that I find myself not afraid to wake up before the sun rises and pray.

Taking the good from the rich friends is not the only advantage to analyzing your circle. But you can make note of the bad ideas, bad habits, and mistakes of those around you and make sure to rid your life of that same thinking. For instance, I am pretty experienced as a graphic designer and though I went to school for it, college only taught me the basics. After college, not only did I go to websites and YouTube to learn techniques and things that I liked, I also collected and studied every flyer, magazine ad, and movie poster that I came across. Most times, I looked for things I would do differently or just flat out better. By paying attention to the bad things that I personally would not do, eventually I had my own style to designing that not only was I satisfied with, but it attracted a lot of good clientele. This helped me to yield great success in the graphic design field.

"Stop wasting time on TV, games, dumb stuff and people, if a person doesn't have a plan….Move on!" ~Tyler Perry on how he became a millionaire

In DreamWorks' movie Turbo, Ryan Reynolds plays the voice of a snail that is obsessed with speed. This snail, of course, lives in an area or small snail village where the norm was to go slow. All that this snail could daydream and think about was going fast. Because of this, all the snails around him laughed at his seemingly pointless and impossible dreams. Eventually, he ran away. Where he lived, no other snail could understand his drive to do something contrary to their reality. He came across a group of snails however, who defied the norm of snails being slow and they loved to race. This opened up a whole new world of dreaming that he didn't even know existed. And now, being surrounded by others who got it, he found himself having bigger goals that landed him in a competition at the Indianapolis 500 against real racecars. Changing his environment and the people (well snails) around him allowed him to achieve the unthinkable. When everyone back at the snail village found out he was racing, no one was laughing anymore.

IRON SHARPENS IRON

"Align yourself with people that you can learn from, people who want more out of life, people who are stretching and searching and seeking some higher ground in life." ~ Les Brown

The quest for success in any area of life, whether it is health, wealth, happiness or spirit, can prove to be unbelievably difficult to figure out. Trying to figure the proper steps and a plan to take is even more difficult to do with other people who have not accomplished what they set out to do. This is why we often hear, *How can the blind lead the blind?* If your goal was to lose weight and have excellent health, would you be more likely to take advice from an overweight friend who you never see at the gym or take advice from The Rock or Terry Crews? If you were starting a business, would you look for advice and investors in your best friend whose landscaping business just brings in 1 or 2 clients a month or rather hear from sharks like Mark Cuban and Lori Greiner?

"A wise man will hear and increase in learning. And a man of understanding will acquire wise counsel." ~ *Proverbs 1:5 KJV*

In just about any field, there is someone who has been there and done that. Although it is not impossible, it can make things more difficult to figure everything by trial and error. Just about any successful person I have researched or came across speaks about having a mentor at some point. Sometimes, it is best that we can humble ourselves enough to ask for help. Why not learn from and listen to the top people in your field or area of choice? As you can see, every example I just gave gives a high profile mentor example, but that doesn't make it impossible at all. In the world we live in, you can find ways to reach anyone, whether it be through social media or flat out emailing them. And if that doesn't work, there are thousands of successful people that have written about what they used and believed, to get them where they wanted to in a book. By purchasing books you can "pick the brain" of these great people, even if they accomplished their success and have passed away. Iron sharpening iron is not just a passage in Proverbs 27, but it means that you may have to be willing to find a friend or mentor or both who is willing to take in your raw form and chip away, tell you truths, and help sharpen you into a sharp and strong metal. Don't look for the person who will agree with your actions and always say yes. Look for a mentor that will lay it to you straight and help you reach dreams or at least take the proper steps to getting closer to your goals.

STEP**SIX**

KEEP GOD IN EVERYTHING

This is probably one of the hardest concepts to fully master. I know that you can be heading to work on a great Monday morning and you have your praise and worship music going, got your mind stayed on Him and all seems to be just fine. Then as soon as you walk in the door at work, a co-worker or the boss seems to have been told by the devil exactly what's needed to get your mind off of God and your focus is disturbed from there on out. For some, it just may be challenging to give God everything. And by everything, I mean everyTHING, including those things you feel God wouldn't "waste time" on. Remember, the bible tells us that He knows the exact count of the hairs on our head. If God can care enough to know something none of us cares to even count or think about, (unless we are going bald), then you rest assured that He is concerned with every aspect of your life, even when you think you are shutting Him out.

I once heard Israel Houghton speak about this subject. He said that a lot of Christians say, "As long as you keep God FIRST...". The problem with that is we sometimes tend to keep God FIRST then go about our daily routine or activities with the satisfaction that we prayed first thing in the morning and thinking that has satisfied God's daily requirement from us. When we actually should keep God in the center of everything; in all of our conversations, daily activities and even thoughts.

"In all your ways acknowledge Him, and He will make your paths straight." ~Proverbs 3:6 KJV

I once had a relationship with a young lady who would always complain that we didn't speak enough. She argued that my attention was with my business and friends. In an attempt to fix the problem, I then began to call first thing in the morning as she was on her way to work, then carry on with my day hoping she was satisfied. Though at first she was good she began to realize that in the mornings was sometimes the only time we really had meaningful conversations. During most of those conversations, I was half asleep. This situation stifled the communication and building of the relationship. How many can relate to having this same kind of communication with God? How can we truly build a relationship with Him speaking to Him just in the mornings or at nights when preparing for bed, or just when He is needed in times of trouble? Keep in mind, He just might want to be kept more than FIRST. Practice keeping Him at the center of EVERYTHING.

"Trust in the LORD with all your heart and do not lean on your own understanding." ~Proverbs 3:5 KJV

Karen Clark Sheard once said in a song, "if you don't see it, before you see it, then you won't see it." I not only found this statement to be powerful, but also very true. There are times where you cannot, or won't be able to physically see things that are set before us. As Christians, we must have faith and lean on God. This includes things that can be as simple as going to a meeting, inquiring about certain business ventures, or where to eat lunch. We previously spoke about that in Proverbs 3:6, it says in ALL your ways acknowledge Him. What we have to realize is that the more we include Him in on everything the easier it will be to trust in him and not rely on our own thoughts and sight.

In the game of football, a lot of people see it as a game of brute strength and hard hitting, but I see a game of much faith. Seemingly, the quarterback throws the ball to a place where there are no receivers, with the expectation that the ball will be caught by a receiver that was en route. Another instance, you will see a player (known as a running back) running into what seems to be a crowd in order to have another player (lineman) who was coming across the field, open up a hole for him to get through. The players on a team must trust each other and like Karen Clark Sheard said, "they have to see it before they can actually see it." That quarterback has to just know his receivers will be where he is throwing the ball and the running back has to know that when he gets to the crowd the lineman will open up the hole. What you don't see is that most successful teams not only have players that spend time on the practice field, but the quarterbacks, the receivers and other players, connect off the field as well. They build relationships outside of the field, which in turn allows them to have faith or trust in each other on the field. So that goes back to our own personal relationship with God. Once we begin to include Him in EVERYTHING and build that relationship with Him, we will see our faith increase. When we are running that route down the field, we know that He is doing what He has promised. When we get 20 yards down the field, the ball will be there. In spiritual terms, once we begin to have that relationship with God, we cannot take the business deal that will have us accepting below our worth but wait for that deal that will move us to another level in what we do. Trust in God and take steps to show it and He will always make a way.

IT DOESN'T HAVE TO BE LONG

Including God in everything is knowing that an acknowledgment (as the scriptures says in Proverbs 3:6, "in all your ways acknowledge Him") can be as simple and quick as to say "Lord, if this is the business deal for me, let me know and make it plain." That one sentence can be the difference of a million dollar deal or a deal that will leave you bankrupt in 5 years. We cannot see the future or what is just right around the corner. If we are in the habit of including God in everything and letting the Holy Spirit guide us, we will find ourselves in less troubles or making bad decisions.

"My son, do not despise the chastening of the LORD, nor detest His correction; for whom the LORD loves He corrects, just as a father the son in whom he delights." ~Proverbs 3:11-12 KJV

A lot of times it's easy to find or see God in the good things that come our way. The promotion on the job, the growing success of our business, the closing on our new home, or our child being on the honor roll. But a lot of the time we might credit the devil with what we deem as bad or uncomfortable situations. Who is to say that us getting that flat tire all of a sudden and having to pull over didn't prevent us from a bad accident. Or by leaving our purses or wallets at home by mistake may have stopped us from over spending.

God makes no mistakes. He is very intentional in his plan and in what he allows to happen. Trust him and keep him involved every step of the way, it will minimize your mistakes and missteps on the path to greatness.

STEP**SEVEN**

JUST OPEN YOUR MOUTH

This is one of my favorite steps!. When it is all said and done, the power that you have in speaking things into existence is boundless but a lot of times overlooked or taken for granted.

> *the power that you have in speaking things into existence is boundless but a lot of times overlooked or taken for granted.*

"…Let the Weak SAY I am Strong!" ~Joel 3:10b KJV

I have a good friend who had a pretty good job at a bank. One day, she lost that job and it just so happened to be the day after she was in a car accident and had her car towed away. She was jobless, without a car and her bills didn't know or care to take a break. As a good friend, I did everything I could and said everything I knew to help motivate her. However, she seemed defeated and it was even harder for her to find another job after countless interviews and bus rides. Her conversation even became defeated and depressed. While on Facebook one day, I noticed that she had changed her tune and she was now posting positive statuses and quotes. I was happy to see that she had found her encouragement. Weeks had gone by and I found myself with some spare time and I gave her a call just to check on her and see how she was doing. She was happy to tell me that she not only had one job offer but two and accepted both. Her problem now wasn't seeing who would hire and accept her, it was now trying to decide which job to turn down. All of this came about when she began to put in the atmosphere positive words and quotes. The seemingly weak SAID I am Strong!

"And the LORD answered me, and said, Write the vision, and make it plain upon tables, that he may run that readeth it. For the vision is yet for an appointed time, but at the end it shall speak, and not lie: though it tarry, wait for it; because it will surely come, it will not tarry."
~Habakkuk 2:2

Many of you know of this great comedian and actor, but what a lot of you do not know is that Jim Carrey once wrote himself a check for acting services rendered. The check was before any major roles and was dated for Thanksgiving 1995 (which at the time of writing the check was 3 years in the future). Just before Thanksgiving 1995, Carrey found out that he would make about 10 million for his role in Dumb and Dumber.

That payday proved to be one of his lowest paydays for a major film since. In fact, his salary doubled in a lot of his movies prior. This all was because of his faith to write a check for how much he wanted to get paid one day and then worked towards it. He essentially *wrote the vision and made it plain.*

MAHUMMAD ALI
TOLD US AND PUT
IT IN THE MEDIA
& WORLD THAT HE
WAS THE GREATEST

GREATEST OF ALL TIME

As I was on YouTube once again, I was looking at random videos, when I came across a video of Michael Jordan, Dikemba Mutombo, & Patrick Ewing having a conversation that Mike had dunked on everyone in the room except Mutombo. He was very adamant that in 6 years in the league, Jordan failed to posterize him. After arguing with Mutombo for a little bit, Jordan said, "Don't worry, it will happen." Later that season Jordan caught a pass on the baseline and fulfilled his prophecy to dunk on Mutombo. Like I once heard Will Smith say, "he who says he can and he who says he can't are both usually right."

Most guys that played with and were close to Michael would agree that he wasn't just a heavy trash talker. He was confident in the affirmations that he spoke through his mouth. He even told Dikemba Mutombo that he would make his last free throw with his eyes closed and he very well did exactly what he said! Sounds crazy right? Death and Life are in the power of the tongue (Proverbs 18:21).

"Joe's gunna come out smokin' and I ain't gunna be jokin'...I'll be peckin' and a pokin', pouring water on his smoking'.... And this might shock and amaze ya but imma destroy." ~Joe Frazier. Muhammad Ali

I know this sounds as crazy as it looks and even as crazy for me to be typing it, but when you hear "greatest of all times" you may think of one or two people. No, not Stephen Reid greatest author of all times, but of course Michael Jordan or Muhammad Ali. Muhammad Ali is very well known for his trash talk and his claiming victory in and out of the ring. He called himself the greatest of all times so much that even decades of boxing later, we cannot erase the fact that he called himself the greatest of all time. His final record was 56–5 but who really even remembers that he lost 5 times. More modern fighters such as Lennox Lewis being 41-2 and even Floyd Mayweather being 49-0 to date have better records. Mahummad Ali told us and put it in the media and world that he was the greatest. He admittedly recognized that he wasn't even known as the biggest, strongest, or fastest fighter. One thing about him, however, is that he never accepted was defeat. He always proclaimed victory over any opponent that he would face in the ring. I believe he won the majority of those fights with the seeds he planted through his words before the actual matches.

I don't find it crazy that two of the greatest of all times are also known as the greatest trash talkers of all times. And I'm not telling you to go through life talking trash but translate this concept over to a winning attitude in life. Speak to your bills, speak into your children, and speak into job interviews. Speak life because at the end of the day, once it is spoken enough, things have no choice but to fall into place.

In 2 Corinthians 4:13 it says "I believed; therefore I have spoken.' Since we have that same spirit of faith, we also believe and therefore speak." We can take on the same spirit of faith as God Himself, whom made us in is own image. He built the world we live in today by just speaking things into existence. When I was younger and would get in trouble (and boy did I get in a lot of trouble), instead of being punished with a belt, my father would often send me to bed and tell me to meditate on my wrong doing. He would tell me to repeat out loud, "I am somebody," until I fell asleep or he was tired of hearing me say it. He was speaking and having me speak over my life, that I was someone greater than the trouble I accepted for myself, someone that would make something of himself. And no, it's not like a magic trick where you say things and they automatically become. I refuse to accept that I am an average person destined for average things. So should you!

> it's not like a magic trick where you say things and they automatically become.

MAKE ROOM FOR SUCCESS

I used to watch MTV cribs, which was a show that allowed you to virtually go into the homes of successful athletes and actors and see how lavishly they lived. What I found really inspiring was not the expensive sports cars or the indoor pools; not even the personal theaters. What intrigued me was that almost every house they went into, the celebrity owned a trophy room. The trophy room was a place set aside to display all of their accomplishments and all of their awards. Hunter's would use trophy rooms to display the creatures they captured. No one on MTV cribs ever said it, but I can only imagine that in their times of feeling low, they could easily lock themselves in this room and see how many beasts they had already conquered. They could see how many platinum records they wrote or see how many Grammy's they won.

But David encouraged himself in the Lord. ~ 1 Samuel 30:6

The key ingredient to pay attention to is that that like David encouraged himself, what better way to do so than focusing on all the good things you have been able to accomplish up until now? Why not make your own trophy room? Create a space where you can come and refocus on your current goals with the positive affirmation that they can be reached because you are surrounded by the end result of previous goals. If you write music and you have the dream of making platinum records, then buy a frame and paint an old record platinum and put it on the wall with your name on it. Let that be there to push and motivate you to have that gold or platinum record. There's nothing wrong with *faith-ing it until you make it,* as long as you're taking steps to actually make it. Set aside a space that you can put up your accomplishments, a place that you can focus on just what you want to accomplish. It might not be a full room now, it may just be a desk drawer with a few certificates in it or a corner of your desk with a trophy on it. But whatever you decide, let it push you, encourage you, and speak to your future goals, to the point where you need more space and bigger goals.

THEY PLAYIN MY SONG

"Music hath charms to soothe the savage beast, to soften rocks, or bend a knotted oak." ~ First line in William Congreve's play The Mourning Bride

If you have not already picked up on it, I am one for watching movies. One thing you will notice in any movie is that the music always accompanies what's happening in the film. Music has a powerful impact on us. It can touch us in ways that words cannot. Music can make you cry, laugh or even make you afraid. Picture going into a club, party or celebration and there was no music or only funeral music, you would probably not feel like dancing, celebrating or partying any longer. Anytime a hero comes into a movie or into a scene to save the day, you hear the most uplifting and triumphant music that makes you think that anything is possible. When I was growing up, one of the most noticeable theme songs was from the movie Shaft. You knew that anytime that music played, every bad guy or situation would come to an end at the hands of Shaft. Simply because he was a bad mutha (shut my mouth). Now if you could have that same effect on negative things that came up against you, or any circumstance that discouraged you, wouldn't that make you just as effective of an overcomer?

I challenge you with this. If every time you wake up, or shower to get your day started, or on your commute, you play songs that speak life and positivity into whatever situation you will face ahead, your problems wouldn't seem so overwhelming. Try to set the tone of your day with a song that makes you feel good. It doesn't necessarily have to be gospel, just positive. I remember running track in college. I would listen to songs like "All I Do is 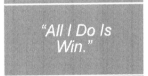 Win" by DJ Khaled, and that worked for me. It gave me the motivation and attitude I needed to face any opponent. Choose what works for you, and to assist, I have included a list of some of my favorite songs I like to set the day with at the end of the book.

WATCH OUT FOR THE NEGATIVE

As I wrote earlier, DEATH and LIFE are in the power of the tongue. It's clear as day in the bible. I'm not just saying someone can speak life but be very aware that DEATH is in the tongue as well. Find a way to build others and build yourself. Don't always accept troubles as they come. One of my prayers is that I will always have more than enough to take care of the things of which I need to take care. I will have more than enough money, wisdom, favor and joy. I will never find myself proclaiming negativity over my life such as I'm broke, poor or depressed! Whenever anyone asked me how I was doing, my response was, "I'm doing GREAT" or at the very least I say, "I will be alright." I try to never speak out negative statements. Even when it is hard, I smile. Try staying mad or sad when you smile, it's almost impossible. So speak life. Don't speak yourself to death. Speak life into others. Speak victoriously. *I am a winner. I am victorious. I am healthy. I am wealthy. I have more than enough. I am beautiful. I am handsome.* Let's speak greatness into ourselves, our families and friends. Positive or negative, if you just speak something long enough, action will follow. Even as you read this book and finish this step, open your mouth and speak some positive things into your life. Pick one area and speak it into your life every day for 21-40 days. If it doesn't change or begin to change then ok, but I can almost guarantee if you speak it, you will achieve it. If you say, "I am in shape. I will lose pounds," eventually, you may just become so motivated to change what you see that you join a gym. Whatever it is, speak it and see where it takes you.

STEP**EIGHT**

NEVER STOP LEARNING

"The mind of the prudent acquires knowledge, And the ear of the wise seeks knowledge." ~ Proverbs 18:15 NASB

In today's world the only thing that seems constant is change itself. We are living in a world where even the apps on our phones are constantly having to be updated. With everything around you always evolving and changing, imagine if you were to stop learning. That's why this step is maybe one of the most vital steps to success and being rich. Almost any job, relationship, or even hobby requires you to never stop learning.

What many people don't know is that many players and teammates confirmed that Michael Jordan was one of the most arrogant players on the court. He talked trash and backed it all up. But one thing that all his coaches agreed on was Jordan being the greatest of all times was yet one of the most coachable players on the court. To be coachable is being open to learning and willing to apply new things, new plays, and new ideas.

"If you are not willing to learn, no one can help you. If you are determined to learn, no one can stop you." *~anonymous*

For many people, once they graduate high school or college, they celebrate the fact that their formal education is over. However, in actuality, the real learning is just beginning. Now is time to get a job, keep that job and even move up in the ranks of the company. It is time to put all the old things you learned into action and you might not realize it, but you are now on a path to constant learning. A lot of successful millionaires and billionaires that we know of today have this one thing in common; it has been called the 5-hour rule. These people deliberately spend at least five hours a week educating themselves. They have accepted the notion that the most effective way to go about learning constantly is to READ, READ, & READ. Inc.com reports that Warren Buffett spends five to six hours per day reading five newspapers and 500 pages of corporate reports. Even with there being only 52 weeks in a year, Bill Gates finds a way to read a minimum of 50 books a year. Mark Zuckerberg reads at least one book every two weeks and no that's not Facebook. My challenge to you is to increase your learning and start reading more. There are people that read for fun and entertainment and there is nothing wrong with that, but let's mix in a couple biographies and begin learn a little about subjects you never thought would interest you. Try setting a goal of how many books you will read a month and by the end of the year increase that number by at least 1 or 2 books.

I have no special talents, I am only passionately curious.
~Albert Einstein

There are other ways of learning that can also help you increase knowledge and worth. I have a friend of mine who is constantly watching documentaries. Consequently, He always has information to give that no one even thinks about. Though it can become annoying to sit through his speeches of knowledge at times, I can say he is rich with knowledge.

You may even want to pick up a hobby. You are not a reader, and don't have time to watch "boring" documentaries; Make time to indulge in a hobby. Learn to put together puzzles or model cars. Learn another language. Learn a sport. Keep your mind in the process of learning. Whether you realize it or not, learning will be a lifelong process. The key to success is to be proactive at learning. Deliberately find new information, and use it, even if it is just in conversation. I have heard it before, that the more you learn the more you'll earn. One of my favorite NFL quarterbacks is the now retired Peyton Manning. Everyone around him knew that it wasn't just his skill set that made him a two time super bowl champ, but the fact that he spent enormous amounts of time learning about the opposing defense, in most cases player by player. He knew certain player's tendencies and key points. Often, the only way teams could beat him was to totally switch up the way they played defense. Even in doing that, it forces the defense to learn and apply more knowledge. In sports and in life, learning is the key to success. Being rich in knowledge will get you the next promotion and take you further than talent can ever take you. Just keep in mind that's the moment you stop learning, that's the moment you become old.

END OF 8 STEPS

THELEGEND

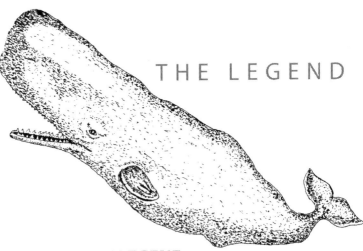

THE LEGEND

REALIZE THE LEGEND
IN YOU. YOU WERE NOT
MADE TO BE CAPTURED
AND/OR HELD BACK BY
PROBLEMS THAT ARE NOT
EVEN ABLE TO MEASURE
UP TO YOUR SIZE.

In the early 1800's sperm whales were hunted because the head of the whale contained a liquid wax called spermaceti. This was used for oil lamps, candles, and other lubricants. Other things from the whales were used in perfumes, soaps, and anything else man could use. So it is safe to say that man saw value in whales and found a great need to hunt and kill these massive creatures.

Whaling boats were the smaller boats that whalers used to harpoon, chase, and capture the whales. These boats in size were generally anywhere between 20 to 30 feet, where a mature male sperm whale could range in size anywhere from 50 to 70 feet. Despite the whale size and strength, they were being captured by the thousands for years, and were threatened by the possibility of extinction.

Now that I have provided you with a little history, this period of time brought along a legendary story. The Essex was a famed whaling ship that was reported to have been sunk by a whale. You might have heard of this whale. He went by the name *Moby Dick.* What made Moby Dick a name and story that is still known today? It wasn't just the awesome penmanship by Herman Melville, though I'm sure it helped. What inspired him to write on such a whale of a tale I think, is something that will help us in our journey to becoming truly rich. As I watched "In the Heart of the Sea," a depiction of the events that took place to sink the Essex in 1820, I realized that Moby Dick hadn't become the legend because he was a beautiful whale that no man could catch. There wasn't anything particularly extraordinary about this whale that made him stand out at face value. Sure, Moby survived harpoon after harpoon, countless ships and crews. However, Moby is a legend because he knew how big he was! He would not allow for ships that weren't even half his size capture and kill him. Instead he struck fear in the hearts of his enemies. He knew that he was bigger and stronger than any of the problems he could see or that he faced.

"Be so good they can't ignore you." ~ Steve Martin

So look deep inside yourself. See just how big God made you to be. Realize the legend in you. You were not made to be captured and/or held back by problems that are not even able to measure up to your size. You might come close to quitting or you might suffer wounds from problems throwing harpoons at you. If you know that you are made to be the legend; people will be speaking about and learning from your story, hundreds of years from now, what can stop you?

> *Realize the legend in you. You were not made to be captured and/or held back by problems that are not even able to measure up to your size.*

IN THE END YOU WIN

Trusting God's ultimate plan for our lives is sometimes very difficult. Often, due to our finite minds, we can only see what we have before us and maybe slightly into our plans for our future. God has a way of turning things around from where we think we can go or are actually heading. If we just make it through to the *end*, we would realize that God had a plan to place us in the winners' circle all along.

Before Jesus began His ministry and beyond, His life was filled with adversity. Being the Son of God on Earth was no walk in the park. From the time He was born, people plotted to take His life. In His adult life, most dignitaries and religious leaders called and treated Jesus like a troublemaker. However, here we find ourselves, over 2000 years later this continues to remain true: anytime someone, whether it be a Christian or non-believer, finds themselves in trouble, being surprised, or in danger, what name almost automatically is screamed out for instant help? Not Stephen, John or even Mary. Troublemaker or not, we call on Jesus!

"No change can happen unless the mindset has first changed."
~T.D. Jakes, on his BET talk show: Mind, Body and Soul

I know that life is life and it is not always easy. You don't always feel like you can win or are even close to winning. You might be facing bill after bill or failure after failure. Bad credit can't seem to get better. Your mega million number didn't hit. Even in all of this, you can still be rich. In this book, I mentioned the word *rich* almost 60 times, but don't lose sight of what it means. Allow these *first* 8 steps to open your mind and change your perspective, which is the first step to changing anything. I was watching a Serena Williams documentary on her 2015 season and she spoke about how she envisioned her and her sister playing each other in Wimbledon, when she was only a kid. Back then, I'm sure it seemed like just a dream. Before she realized it, she first imagined it and the mindset took over from there.

IF IT AIN'T ABOUT THE MONEY

"17 And when he was gone forth into the way, there came one running, and kneeled to him, and asked him, Good Master, what shall I do that I may inherit eternal life? 18 And Jesus said unto him, Why callest thou me good? there is none good but one, that is, God. 19 Thou knowest the commandments, Do not commit adultery, Do not kill, Do not steal, Do not bear false witness, Defraud not, Honour thy father and mother. 20 And he answered and said unto him, Master, all these have I observed from my youth. 21 Then Jesus beholding him loved him, and said unto him, One thing thou lackest: go thy way, sell whatsoever thou hast, and give to the poor, and thou shalt have treasure in heaven: and come, take up the cross, and follow me. 22 And he was sad at that

saying, and went away grieved: for he had great possessions. 23 And Jesus looked round about, and saith unto his disciples, How hardly shall they that have riches enter into the kingdom of God! 24 And the disciples were astonished at his words. But Jesus answereth again, and saith unto them, Children, how hard is it for them that trust in riches to enter into the kingdom of God! 25 It is easier for a camel to go through the eye of a needle, than for a rich man to enter into the kingdom of God. 26 And they were astonished out of measure, saying among themselves, Who then can be saved? 27 And Jesus looking upon them saith, With men it is impossible, but not with God: for with God all things are possible." ~ Mark 19: 17-27 KJV

Even though I entitled this section with the chorus of the rappers, TI and Young Thug's song, my thinking is actually pretty contrary. In this brief encounter and short passage of about 10 verses. This rich man comes up to Jesus and tells him that he has upheld the Ten Commandments since his youth. Jesus however, tells him that the one thing he actually lacks in is something that he has a lot of: his riches and possessions. By this, Jesus tells him to give away all his riches to the poor and join them on their walk to spread the gospel. I believe Jesus was summing up almost every step in this book. He told the man to give to the poor, put his trust in God and to learn how to live without all of his prized possessions. He was saying that being rich is not about money at all and if you don't get this, you don't get it at all. He explained to His disciples that great reward comes to those who understand this concept and that with God all things are possible. I see why this man was a great teacher. He put in 10 verses what I am putting in an entire book. Whether you take it from this book or from the 10 scriptures, I want you to know that being rich "ain't all about the money."

RECAP

There is no set amount of rules or steps to getting rich. For some, it might take 67 steps or 12 or 15. But I know that in these steps you will begin to move closer to that end result of total fulfillment. Again, it's not even about obtaining money because you can be rich in finances and still lack in other major areas in life. Once you begin to always give, believe in yourself, stop being lazy, fully trust God, choose your friends, keep God involved, speak it, and never stop earning, there is no way you can remain on the same level. And as you read this, I am already preparing to give you a second group of steps to richness, steps towards finishing strong, being proactive, thinking big, and finding balance will all be included in the second book to this series. For now, let's focus on the first 8 steps. We are all on journey to pursuing happiness and being better.

SET YOUR ATMOSPHERE

When I personally faced situations that called for me to encourage myself or change my atmosphere, I have leaned on music, books, and movies to help push me to that change I may have needed. I ran track for about 10 years of my life. Often before my races I would find myself listening to various songs to get me ready for a competition. I have found myself in positions where I turned to the bible for motivation and answers. I have read books that changed my thinking and helped to motivate me to seek more. Instead of leaving you to find your own I want to share a list of these things with you. This is my personal list of things that have helped me. You may find that they help you and in that case use them and allow them to motivate you and help you on this journey that we are on to being truly rich.

> *We are all on journey to pursuing happiness and being better.*

APPENDIX

SCRIPTURES

Try committing these verses to memory, speaking them out loud until they actually change your situation or help you in your thinking:

Psalms 150:6 - Praise ye the Lord
Psalms 118:24 - This is the Day
Psalms 82:4 - Poor 7 Needy
Psalms 81:1 - Sing Aloud
Psalms 46:1 - Refuge & Strength
Psalms 34:1 - My Mouth
Psalms 47:1 - Clap Your Hands
Psalms 48:1 - Great is the Lord
Psalms 41:1 - Considers the Poor
Psalms 25:2 - OMG I Trust
Psalms 27:1 - Who shall I Fear
Psalms 25:4 - Ways O'God
Psalms 19:14 - Words of My Mouth
Psalms 1:1 - Blessed is the Man
Psalms 2:11 - Serve the Lord
Psalms 24:1 - Earth is the Lord's
Psalms 34:8 - Taste & See
Psalms 3:8 - Salvation Belongs
Psalms 103:1 - I Will Bless The Lord

Psalms 88:1-2 - God of My Salvation
Psalms 51: 10-11 - Create In Me
Psalms 118:8 - Trust God
Psalms 18:2 - Lord is My Rock
Psalms 21:13 - Be Exalted
Psalms 118:1 - Oh Give Thanks
Psalms 100:1-5 - Joyful Noise
Proverbs 3:5-6 - All thy Heart
James 1:22 - Be Ye Doers
Romans 14:16 - Good Not Evil
Philippians 4:13 - All Things
2 Corinthians 10:4-5 No Weapons
2 Corinthians 12:9 - My Grace
Romans 3:23 - All Have Sinned
Philippians 4:6 - Anxious for Nothing
Philippians 4:7 - Peace of God
1 Peter 5:10-11 God of Grace
Deuteronomy 30:19 - Chose Life
Mark 11:22-24 - Faith in God
Romans 8:6 - Spiritually Minded

SONGS

Earlier in this book we spoke about theme songs and how to let songs set you atmosphere for the day. These are songs I use to encourage or make me feel better. While I shower, I'll play them or when I'm driving I'll have them in my playlist or just put one on repeat:

Jason Nelson - Don't Count Me Out
Twinkie Clark - God's Got A Blessing
Kirk Franklin - I Am
Jason Nelson - I Am
Travis Greene - Made A Way
DJ Khalid - All I Do Is Win
Panic At The Disco - Victorious
Jason Nelson - Dominion
Dottie Peoples - On Time God
Marvin Sapp - He Saw The Best In Me
Dewayne Woods - Let Go

BOOKS

The more that you read, the more things you will know. The more that you learn, the more places you'll go. ~ Dr. Seuss

The more you read, you will equip yourself with the knowledge and everything it takes to reach success and true richness in life. Here are a few books to keep on your list. They will inspire and inform you, but don't let it stop there find other books to read.

Unlimited Power - Tony Robbins
Start Where You Are - Chris Gardner
Act Like A Success, Think Like A Success -Steve Harvey
Think And Grow Rich - Napoleon Hill
Super Rich - Russell Simmons

Live Your Dreams - Les Brown
Made In America - Sam Walton
Become A Better You - Joel Osteen
You Can You Will - Joel Osteen
Reposition Yourself - TD Jakes
Total Recall - Arnold Schwarzenegger

REFERENCES

FailVideos."Dog Won't Walk Through Door Fail" Online Video Clip. Youtube. 27 Nov, 2015. Web. 23 Dec, 2015

Simon Dodson. "Dikembe Mutombo Michael Jordan" Online Video Clip. Youtube. 13 May, 2013. Web. 23 Nov, 2015

Tour. "Michael Jordan Famous Eyes Closed Free Throw to Mutombo In Full" Online Video Clip. Youtube. 27 June, 2011. Web. 23 Nov, 2015

Iconic. "Muhammad Ali engaging in some of his famous trash talk" Online Video Clip. Youtube. 11 Nov, 2010. Web. 25 Nov, 2015

Documentary History Channel. "The Electric Light History | Thomas Edison Inventions | Documentary History Film" Online Video Clip. Youtube. 26 Jan, 2015. Web. 25 May, 2015

IAC Publishing Labs, 2014, "What percentage of Americans are millionaires?", https://www.reference.com/business-finance/percentage-americans-millionaires-c3a30edf68c8c4d5#

Robert N. Fried & Cary Woods (Producers), & David Anspaugh (Director). (1993). Rudy [Motion

Picture]. United States: TriStar Pictures.
Lisa Stewart (Producer), & David Soren (Director). (2013). Turbo [Motion Picture]. United States: DreamWorks Animation.

Brian Grazer, Ron Howard, Will Ward, Joe Roth, Paula Weinstein
(Producer), & Ron Howard (Director). (2015). In the Heart of the Sea [Motion Picture]. United States: Warner Bros. Pictures.

John Singleton (Producer)(Director). (2001). Baby Boy [Motion Picture]. United States: Columbia Pictures.

money.cnn.com/2015/02/11/news/companies/lottery-spending/
February 11, 2015

ACKNOWLEDGEMENTS

I never thought of myself as an author. I now know that it's something that God considered me to be before I was born. I would like to first thank God for seeing in me something I couldn't see in myself.

There was one person who was there when I came to the reality that I would actually accept the things that I feel God was placing inside of me to give to the world in this book, Rondell Riddle. Thank you for helping me believe in myself and always listening to the early chapters of this book, even when it was late night and we were sleepy.

I would like to also thank Amira, Waheebah, Auntie Robin, and Auntie Shaun (even though I never emailed you) for reading and proofreading at different stages of this book. I would also like to thank Danielle and Dwayne Jennings. You both have been a true blessing to me and my family. You always told me like it is and never looked to take advantage of me and my talents. GO BLUE EDEN!!!!

Thank you Ana Mercedes for being one person I truly couldn't have written this book without. You really helped make this happen and I am grateful.

Meshele Scipio thanks for not allowing me publish foolery, you changed everything at the expense of genuine kindness. I appreciate you greatly.

I would like to thank Antione, Lenny, Quan, & Joe (My Hittas) for being there when I went through some of my toughest times and always encouraging me to always move forward.

Behind every great man is an even greater woman. And I am very privileged to be able to thank Jihan (GG) for not always agreeing with me, but telling me what was best. Thank you for believing in me and pushing me to finish this project.

Now that I put my "boo" in my book I would like to thank you Cynthia Reid. Mom I mentioned to you what I was doing and let you read a little and you was automatically on board. That encouraged me to make it really happen and not throw it to the side. Thank you for simply believing in your favorite and first born son. LOVE YOU.

A Seton Hall University graduate, Stephen Reid is a multi-talented individual who is originally born in Gary, IN. and raised in Atlanta, GA. While in school at Seton Hall he studied and received his BA in Communications with a concentration in Graphic/Web Design.

Since becoming a self-employed graphic/web designer he has worked with various talents and artists in the entertainment industry such as Erica Campbell, Hezekiah Walker, Tye Tribbett, Timiney Figueroa, JJ Hairston and many more.

In 2010, Stephen added photography to his arsenal of weapons in the industry. He is now an up and coming celebrity photographer who has also shot still photography for *E! Entertainment*. He has shot celebrities such as Kathy Lee Gifford, Kelly Price, Rickey Smiley, B Slade (formally known as Tonex), Lahlah Hathaway and more.

Now in 2017, he is adding the titles, author and motivational speaker to his belt. With this freshman publication, he is spreading his message and inspiring the world to be truly rich.

42280023R00086

Made in the USA
Middletown, DE
07 April 2017